unTime® Piano

agtime & Marches

T0086903

Level 3A–3B

Easy Piano

Arranged by

Nancy and Randall Faber

Production Coordinator: Jon Ophoff
Design and Illustration: Terpstra Design, San Francisco
Engraving: Dovetree Productions, Inc.

FABER
PIANO ADVENTURES®
3042 Creek Drive
Ann Arbor, Michigan 48108

A NOTE TO TEACHERS

FunTime® Piano Ragtime & Marches offers immense appeal to the piano student with this collection of ever-popular pieces from the early 1900s. In addition to being excellent supplementary material, the pieces are useful for recital or other performance.

FunTime® Ragtime & Marches is part of the *FunTime Piano* series. "FunTime" designates Level 3 of the *PreTime® to BigTime® Piano Supplementary Library* arranged by Faber and Faber.

Following are the levels of the supplementary library, which lead from *PreTime to BigTime*.

PreTime® Piano	(Primer Level)
PlayTime® Piano	(Level 1)
ShowTime® Piano	(Level 2A)
ChordTime® Piano	(Level 2B)
FunTime® Piano	(Level 3A–3B)
BigTime® Piano	(Level 4)

Each level offers books in a variety of styles, making it possible for the teacher to offer stimulating material for every student. For a complimentary detailed listing, e-mail faber@pianoadventures.com or write us at the mailing address below.

Visit us at **PianoAdventures.com**.

Helpful Hints:

1. In both "rags" and marches, rhythm is of prime importance. Stress a steady left hand that does not overpower the right hand melody. Hands-alone practice is helpful.

2. Most of the rags are arranged in cut time. The use of quarter and half notes in place of eighth and quarter notes makes the ragtime syncopation more accessible. While the student may begin at a slower practice tempo, it is important that he/she work up to the metronome marking at the beginning of the piece.

3. It is beneficial for the teacher to play and/or record the piece for the student. This helps familiarize the student with the ragtime or march style.

About Ragtime and Marches

The march was very popular with the brass bands and dance bands of the late 1800s and was made even more popular with the success of John Philip Sousa's patriotic marches. Pianists often played arrangements of marches and other popular music. A style developed where the pianist would spice up the melody of these songs by using a syncopated rhythm (playing between the strong beats), while keeping a steady left hand. This became known as "ragging" the melody, and eventually developed into a style of its own called "Ragtime." Ragtime and marches have a number of characteristics in common, including similar harmony, regular phrases, and strongly marked rhythm.

ISBN 978-1-61677-008-2

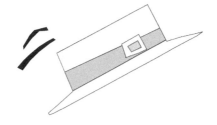

TABLE OF CONTENTS

The Entertainer

By SCOTT JOPLIN

Snowflake Rag

By NANCY FABER

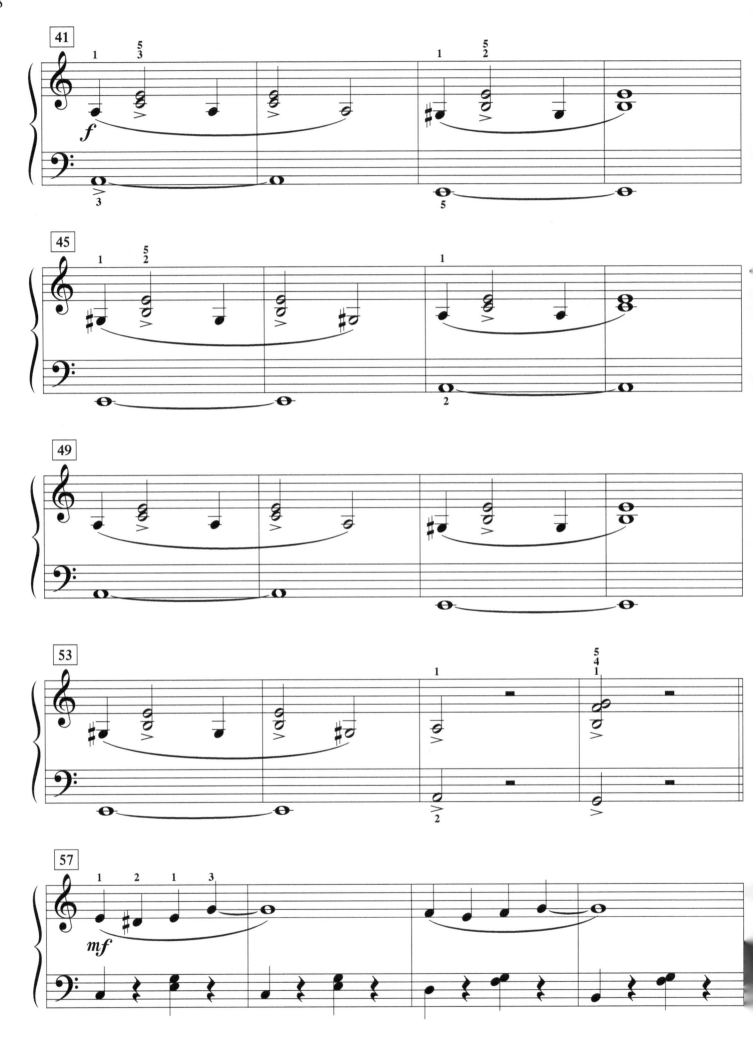

When the Saints Go Marching In

TRADITIONAL

saints   go   march - ing   in.

The Easy Winners

By SCOTT JOPLIN

14

Pineapple Rag

By SCOTT JOPLIN

The Stars and Stripes Forever

By JOHN PHILIP SOUSA

With a bounce

Maple Leaf Rag

By SCOTT JOPLIN

Parade of the Tin Soldiers

By LEON JESSEL

Graceful march tempo

The Ants Came Marching

TRADITIONAL

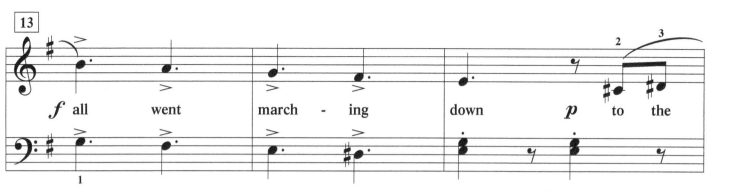

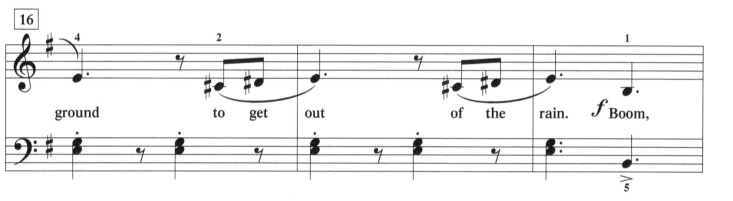

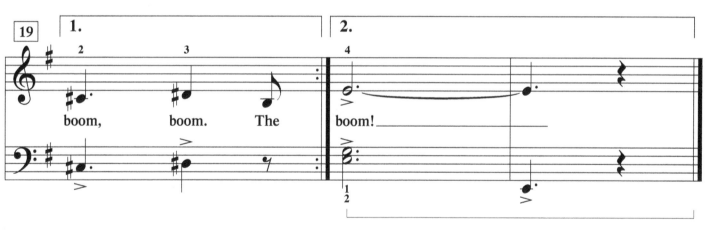

2. The ants came marching two by two, Hurrah! Hurrah!
The ants came marching two by two, Hurrah! Hurrah!
The ants came marching two by two,
The little one stopped to tie his shoe. And they all went marching
Down to the ground to get out of the rain. (Boom, boom, boom.)

3. The ants came marching three by three…
   The little one stopped to climb a tree…

4. The ants came marching four by four…
   The little one stopped to shut the door…

5. The ants came marching five by five…
   The little one stopped to take a dive…

6. The ants came marching six by six…
   The little one stopped to pick up sticks…

7. The ants came marching seven by seven…
   The little one stopped to go to heaven…

8. The ants came marching eight by eight…
   The little one stopped to shut the gate…

9. The ants came marching nine by nine…
   The little one stopped to scratch his spine…

10. The ants came marching ten by ten…
    The little one stopped to say *The end*…

Glad Cat Rag

By WILL NASH

American Patrol

By F. W. MEACHAM

Strict march beat